JavaScript

JavaScript Programming Made Easy for Beginners & Intermediates

(Step By Step With Hands On Projects)

Craig Berg

Introduction

JavaScript is a lightweight, interpreted programming language and client-side scripting language that's normally used to manipulate the behavior of components in a web page. The manipulation that JavaScript provides helps improve the functionality of the website or web application.

JavaScript is one among many other web scripting languages such as ActionScript, Perl Script, PHP, among various others. With that noted though, JavaScript is one of the most popular scripting languages, which is why many programmers usually refer to it as the "language of the web."

JavaScript integrates well with HTLM and CSS to create responsive and interactive web applications, which is why it has become a MUST learn scripting language for every software developer and if you are especially interested in working in Web Development Aspects, you need to master JavaScript.

This does however not mean that JavaScript web development is the only way to use JavaScript. You can also use it to build standalone web applications that run on the browser. And the good thing is that JavaScript has simple requirements and setup process.

The following are some of the features that make JavaScript popular and a programming language every programmer should learn:

- ✓ It is used in web and mobile application development,

JavaScript

- ✓ It is a scripting language interpreted by an engine,
- ✓ It is an Object Oriented Programming language,
- ✓ It helps create beautiful and fast web applications,
- ✓ It offers Standard implementation,
- ✓ It is dynamic and fast,
- ✓ JavaScript is cross platform,
- ✓ Used to create both front-end and back-end applications.

JavaScript has no relationship with Java; the only similarity between the two is that some of the keywords and syntax may be alike. Nevertheless, the two languages are unrelated.

JavaScript is a broad language that has a ton tons of frameworks and libraries. The following are the most popular of these frameworks and libraries:

- ✓ Node.JS
- ✓ Angular JS
- ✓ React
- ✓ JQuery
- ✓ Polymer JS
- ✓ Vue.js
- ✓ Backbone JS
- ✓ Aurelia

JavaScript

The following are some of JavaScript programming language features we shall be discussing in this guide and using hands-on projects, show you how to use JavaScript to create dynamic, responsive web pages and web applications:

- ✓ **It supports Server-Side Programming** – In programming, we normally use frameworks such as Node.js to deploy complex JavaScript server applications.
- ✓ **Asynchronous back-end** – JavaScript provides frameworks such as Ajax to help with back-end data loading while performing other tasks.
- ✓ **HTML manipulation** – JavaScript aids the process of manipulating HTML web pages.
- ✓ **Input Validation** – Programmers and web developers normally use JavaScript to verify the user inputs in the browser before submitting.

In this JavaScript guide for beginners and intermediates, you shall learn everything you need to learn to go from having very little knowledge of how to use JavaScript, to being someone who can use JavaScript to create a dynamic, web-based game that has two levels of difficulty: easy and difficult.

PS: Don't forget to leave a review of this book on Amazon if you like it!

Table of Content

Introduction 2

Chapter 1: JavaScript ECMAScript Standard 10

   A Brief History of JavaScript............................. 10

   Environment Setup 12

Chapter 2: Working With JavaScript: A Brief HTML Guide for Beginners... 14

   HTML Basic Structure 14

   The Script Tag 16

Chapter 3: Working with JavaScript: A Brief CSS Guide for Beginners 18

   CSS Overlay 18

Chapter 4: Introduction to JavaScript Syntax 21

   JavaScript Comments 22

   White Spaces, Semicolons, and Line breaks 23

Chapter 5: Working with JavaScript Variables 25

   Variable Naming Conventions 26

   Scope Variables in JS 27

   JavaScript Keywords 27

Chapter 6: Working With JavaScript Data Types .. 30

    JavaScript Numbers 31

    JavaScript Booleans 31

    Strings in JavaScript 32

    Null in JavaScript 35

    Javascript Undefined 35

    Time – JavaScript 36

    JavaScript Arrays 37

    JavaScript Objects 39

Chapter 7: Working with JavaScript Operators 42

    Arithmetic Operators 43

    Assignment Operators 45

    Comparison Operators 47

    Boolean/Logical Operators 49

    Bitwise Operators 51

    Conditional Operators 52

Chapter 8: Working with JavaScript Conditionals 54

    If Conditions 54

If...Else 55

Else...if 56

JavaScript Switch 58

Chapter 9: Working with JavaScript Loops 60

JavaScript For Loops 60

JavaScript While Loops 61

Do...While Loops 62

Chapter 10: Working with JavaScript Functions ... 64

Function Definition 64

Function Calls 65

Function Parameters 65

Return Value 66

JavaScript Nested Functions 66

Anonymous Functions 67

Chapter 11: Working with JavaScript Events 68

Onclick Event 68

OnMouseOver and onMouseOut Events 69

Chapter 12: About Different Types of Errors & JavaScript Error Handling 72

JavaScript

Types of Program Errors 72

Syntax Errors 72

Runtime Errors 73

Logical Errors 73

The JavaScript Error Handling Mechanism 73

JavaScript Throw Statement............................... 75

Chapter 13: JavaScript's Document Object Model 76

DOM Methods 78

DOM Document Object 79

Chapter 14: Asynchronous JavaScript and XML (AJAX) 82

XMLHttpRequest Object – Ajax.......................... 84

XMLHttpRequest Methods 84

XMLHttpRequest Properties 85

Chapter 15: Forms and Form Validations Using JavaScript 87

Basic Form Validation 87

Data Form Validation 88

Chapter 16: JavaScript Project: Step By Step Process to Create the Color Game 90

Conclusion... 107

Check Out My Other Books 108

Chapter 1: JavaScript ECMAScript Standard

ECMAScript is a conventional specification for scripting languages regulated by the ECMA International. It is core to several scripting languages such as JavaScript, ActionScript, and Jscript.

In this guide, we are not going to look at the history of the ES standardization. What we are going to do is use the ECMAScript to learn a bit more about the evolution of JavaScript.

You can however learn more about the ECMAScript standard by visiting the following resource page:

https://bit.ly/2DZiHQb

A Brief History of JavaScript

JavaScript is the creation of Brendan Eich, who at the time of creating the scripting language, was an employee at Netscape Communications Corporation, a corporation that Wikipedia notes had hired him to help embed their *"schema programming language into the Netscape Navigator, one of the most dominant web browser of the 1990s."*

Wikipedia also notes that before Eich could start his work at Netscape in 1995, the company collaborated with Sun Microsystems with the former agreeing to use Sun's static programming language, Java, in their Netscape Navigator.

JavaScript developed out of the collaboration mentioned above because once Netscape Communications and Sun's Microsystem collaborated, Netscape Communications immediately realized that they needed to create a new scripting language whose syntax was similar to that of Java so that the two languages could complement each other well and allow Netscape to create web technologies platforms that could effectively compete with Microsoft, one of the giant computing companies of the 1990s.

Netscape tasked Eich with the task of creating a prototype of this scripting language, which is how, as Wikipedia notes, Eich ended up creating JavaScript in 10 days of May 1995.

During its developmental stages in the 1990s, JavaScript went by the name Mocha, and during its beta development stages in Netscape Navigator 2.0, it was initially called LiveScript a name later changed to JavaScript in December 1995 with the intent behind the name not being to cause confusion or to mean that the language was similar to Java, but to capitalize on the popularity of Java—and Java was the most popular programming language of the time.

JavaScript follows the script version released and maintained by the ECMAScript. In this book, we are going to focus on illustration based on the latest version of JavaScript i.e. ECMA 2019 which has significant improvements over the previous versions.

JavaScript

Environment Setup

In this section, we are going to look at some of the tools we are going to use to write programs in JavaScript. JavaScript does not offer complex working environment; to work with it effectively, all you truly need is a **text editor** and a ***browser***.

For the tutorials in this JavaScript guidebook, we are going to use the Latest version of Google chrome as our web browser of choice and the Brackets Text Editor as our text editor of choice for the various illustrations you are going to find in this guide. You can download these two pieces of software from the following resource pages:

https://www.google.com/chrome/

http://brackets.io/

You can use any text editor or browser you feel comfortable working with. To enable the JavaScript console in your browser, Right click inside your browser and select "developer options" then navigate to console.

NOTE: To learn how to use JavaScript to create dynamic and responsive web pages and applications, you need to have some knowledge of how the web works, as well as how to work with HTML and CSS.

JavaScript

The next chapter of the guide will briefly introduce you to HTML and show you how to work with it so that you can couple it, JavaScript, and CSS to create amazing web applications and products.

Chapter 2: Working With JavaScript: A Brief HTML Guide for Beginners

In this chapter, we are going to look at some of the basic HTML elements you need to understand in order to learn JavaScript as well as comprehend the contents as well as the various hands-on tutorials in this JavaScript book.

NOTE: This is not a HTML tutorial. It is simply a basic introduction to working with HTML because to become learn JavaScript and to become efficient at using JavaScript to create web applications and pages, you need to having some basic knowledge of how to work with HTML.

HTML, which stands for Hyper Text Markup Language, is a markup language that we normally use to define the structure of a web document such as headings, sub-headings, paragraphs and such. Since it developed at the advent of the World Wide Web, HTML is old and has advanced and changed significantly over the years. Today, we normally use HTML to format web documents for the purpose of sharing information.

To equip you with the basic HTML knowledge you need to have to start working with JavaScript effectively, we are going to look at several key aspects of a HTML document:

HTML Basic Structure

All HTML documents have a standard structure, also called the basic boilerplate. The following tags are in most documents that appear as html.

JavaScript

```
<!DOCTYPE html>
<html>
    <head>
        <title></title>
    </head>
    <body>
    </body>
</html>
```

Let us explore the document above.

- The **<!DOCTYPE html>** in html is not a primitive HMTL tag (discussed later). We use it to alert the browser of the version the HTML document is using. The syntax for the doctype for HTML 5 and HTML 4 is different. <!DOCTYPE html> is essential and should always be at the start of any html document.

- The **html tag** – This is the root tag for the entire html document. All other tags within the html document must be within the html tag.

- The **<head>** – In an html document, we use the head tag as a container for the metadata to be found on the web page. We place this tag after the html tag and before the body tag.

- The **body tag** – We use this tag to represent the beginning of an html document body. Not all tags go here, but almost every other tag such as images, text, and other media in the document are within these tags.

- The **title tag** – We use this tag to set the title of the HTML document. We place this title within the opening and closing title tag as <title>Title page</title>

JavaScript

NOTE: Most html tags require 'closing.' HTML5 and some browser may recognize unclosed tag and fix it. However, getting into the habit of always closing tags that require closing is a good way to improve your programming skills.

The Script Tag

Now that we have introduced the concept of tags, let us look at the most important HTML tag we are going to use in the book, ***the script tag.***

We normally use the script tag <script></script> to include client-side scripts such as JavaScript code. The opening and closing of the script tag may contain a reference to an external JavaScript file or can include native JavaScript code within it. We can classify this tag as a document metadata.

The script tag also accepts other attributes. Let us look at the **src** attribute that allows you to specify the location of the external script file. For example, fire up your text editor and type in the following code. Remember that for the tutorials in this guide, we shall be using Brackets:

```
<!DOCTYPE html>
<html>
    <script src="/Files/index.js"></script>
    <head>
        <title></title>
    </head>
    <body>
    </body>
</html>
```

This script tells the browser to locate the file in the Files directory, under the name index.js file. A script may have many other attributes; we have merely used this to illustrate

JavaScript

the most important HTML tag whose knowledge of use you need to have before you can create JavaScript webpages and applications.

NOTE: As mentioned earlier, you cannot use JavaScript without some knowledge of HTML and CSS.

Now that you have some basis knowledge of the most important HTML tags you need to know to work with HTML and JavaScript, the next chapter of the guide shall give you a brief introduction to CSS so that you can combine the three web programming languages to create dynamic webpages and applications.

Chapter 3: Working with JavaScript: A Brief CSS Guide for Beginners

Cascading Style Sheet or CSS is a design language used to present and modify the appearance of web pages. It allows web developers to change page features such as the fonts, image presentation and locations of various html elements. HTML, CSS and JavaScript work together, which is why in this section of the guidebook, we are going to look at the basics of working with CSS so that it is not a foreign term within the book or to you as we delve deeper into learning JavaScript in later chapters of the book.

Like HTML, JavaScript, PHP, Python, and other programming languages, CSS evolves with time with new features added every time and with each evolution. This book focuses on the latest version of CSS i.e. CSS3.

CSS Overlay

CSS files are linked externally on the html page. However, you can include the CSS code within the HTML (inline CSS) but we do not recommend that. CSS code has three main parts.

It comprises of a set of rules that mainly focus on the styling part, which are then interpreted by the browser, and then applied to their respective elements.

CSS's three main parts are:

JavaScript

- **A selector** – The CSS selector is a HTML tag that the styling is applied to. It could be a paragraph (using <p> tag).

- **Property** – A property is an attribute of an HTML tag. The properties include: colors, borders, navigations, etc.

- **Value** – values are defined values assigned to variables. The border could be 2px wide. The 2px is the value assigned to the border property.

A typical CSS syntax is:

Selector: {

    Property: value;

    Property2: value;

}

```
h1 {
    color: aquamarine;
    border-bottom: 2px;
}
p {
    font-family: "Times New Roman", Times, serif;
}
```

From the above example, the h1 and p, which represent the heading one and paragraph respectively, represent the selector. Next, once we select the element we want to manipulate, we can set properties and values such as color and set it to blue, red, or aquamarine. In colors, you can set it in RGB or HEX code.

They are many types of CSS selectors and selection methods. For example, you can use the * (asterisk) as a global selector. You can also use the element id to select a specific element in case there are multiple.

NOTE: This is not a CSS book and CSS is therefore beyond the scope of this book. What this chapter sought to do is give you a basic understanding of the most important CSS elements you need to know how to use in order to start learning how to create JavaScript code, web pages, and web applications too.

Now that you have a basic understanding of how to work with HTML and CSS, we can move on to learning how to work with JavaScript as you pursue mastery of this important scripting language especially if your intention is to learn JavaScript so that you can create dynamic webpages and responsive web applications and websites.

Chapter 4: Introduction to JavaScript Syntax

In this section, we are going to look at the basics of JavaScript syntax and learn how to create our first JavaScript program.

We implement JavaScript using the <script></script> tags in HTML web page. We can place a script tag anywhere in the web page. However, it is usually better to place the tag within the <head></head> tags of your web page. Once the browser comes across the <script> tags within a page, it automatically loads the JavaScript code into the web page.

Below is the basic syntax of how a JavaScript code loads onto a web page.

```
<html>
  <body>
    <script language = "javascript" type = "text/javascript">
      <!--
        document.write("Hello World!")
      //-->
    </script>
  </body>
</html>
```

From the above code, we see that the script tag features 2 very important attributes namely: The **language attribute** used to specify the name of the scripting language that has been used used in the file, and the *s* used to show the use of the scripting language.

We include the HTML comments around the Javascript code incase the browser running the code does not support

JavaScript. Next, we call the write function that writes the text "Hello World" in the HTML document.

We can write JavaScript code inside the HTML file as shown above —not recommended— or we can link it to an external JavaScript file saved on a different location as shown below.

```
<html>
  <body>
    <script type="text/javascript" src="index.js"></script>
  </body>
</html>
```

The index.js file specified above will contain the Javascript code as shown below.

```
alert("Hello world");
```

JavaScript Comments

JavaScript uses the C and C++ commenting style where:

- o JavaScript ignores the Text between the two forward slashes // to the end of the line is.

- o We use the /* comment */ syntax for multi-line commenting.

- o Supports the HTML open comment syntax that we normally use as a single line comment <!--

- o JavaScript does not recognize the HTML closing comment tag and is closed by use of //->

JavaScript

```
<html>
    <body>
        <script type="text/javascript">
            <!--
                // c, c++ single line commenting
                /* multi
                *
                *line commenting
                */
                //-->
        </script>
    </body>
</html>
```

White Spaces, Semicolons, and Line breaks

Like most programming languages, JavaScript ignores whitespaces such as tabs, spaces, and newlines. JavaScript allows the use of these features to format and organize the code. This makes the code easy to read and understand.

Unlike C++, C and Java in JavaScript, Semicolons are optional. It is however a good practice to end every JavaScript statement with a semi colon. For example, if you declaring variables in the same line, it will result into an error.

```
<html>
    <body>
        <script type="text/javascript">
            <!--
                // semicolon not required
                var 10
                var 100
                // semicolons required
                var 10; var 100;
                //-->
        </script>
    </body>
</html>
```

JavaScript

JavaScript is case-sensitive and requires that all identifiers such as variable names, functions, and keywords be typed with capitalization of letters. For example, the name `VarName` and `varName` are not the same.

JavaScript

Chapter 5: Working with JavaScript Variables

Similar to other programming languages, JavaScript supports variables. Variables are storage entities within a computer program. We usually use them to store information that will be necessary later in program.

We can relate variable to pronouns in the English language. Once you declare a variable, you can reference to it by calling its name. JavaScript requires you to declare a variable before using it. In JavaScript, The syntax for variable declaration is as follows:

`<var> <variable_name> = <value>`

Variable initialization, which is setting of the value of the specified variable, is not necessary in variable declaration. For example, you can create a variable called myName and later set the value to "James" when you need it.

```html
<html>
    <body>
        <script type="text/javascript">
            <!--
            var firstName = "Green";
            var myName;

            myName = "James";
            //-->
        </script>
    </body>
</html>
```

In the latest versions (ES6 and above) of JavaScript, you can declare a variable using the **let** keyword or the **var** keywords

JavaScript

or the **const**. The var and let keywords have similar functions with differences in the scope constraints. Once you declare a variable using the var or let keyword, you cannot redeclare it.

JavaScript variables cannot support any data type which means that JavaScript is an un-typed language. Unlike languages such as Java or C++ where you have to specify the data type, JavaScript automatically detects this.

JavaScript variable values can change during program execution; the good thing is that JavaScript performs the variable update automatically.

Variable Naming Conventions

JavaScript has a set of rules that apply when it comes to creating a name for your variable. The most important of these rules are as follows:

- A Variable name should not be a keyword
- The first letter of the variable name should be a dollar sign, an underscore or a letter.
- The subsequent characters after the first letter can be a number, a letter, a dollar sign or an underscore.
- As noted above, JavaScript variable names are case-sensitive.

Scope Variables in JS

Variable scope refers to the area of the program where a variable is accessible directly without conflicts. JavaScript offers two main types of variable scopes:

- Local Scope – accessibility within the function being executed.

- Global Scope – Accessible anywhere within the JavaScript program and functions.

Within the defined function, a local variable scope takes a higher precedence over a global variable scope if it contains the same name. For example, if you declare a variable with a global scope called myName and then declare a variable with the same name in a function, once you call a function, the local variable will be what the program uses.

```html
<html>
    <body onload = checkscope();>
        <script type = "text/javascript">
        <!--
            var myName = "JavaScript Global";     // global variable
            function scope( ) {
                var myName = "Happy JavaScripting";   // local variable
                document.write(myVar); // function call within scope function
            }
        //-->
        </script>
    </body>
</html>
```

If we type and run the above code, it prints "Happy JavaScripting" This is because the local variable receives a higher precedence.

JavaScript Keywords

In this section, we are going to look at some of the most common JavaScript keywords that you cannot use as variable identifiers, method, function names, or objects. Some will be similar to those found in other programming languages:

JavaScript

abstract	extends	export	protected
with	native	goto	this
switch	private	volatile	function
Boolean	null	void	true
break	new	throws	for
False	if	private	synchronized
finally	const	char	class
short	static	return	in
super	package	while	enum
double	do	debugger	import

Chapter 6: Working With JavaScript Data Types

JavaScript and other scripting languages such as Python and Ruby fall under a category of programming languages referred to as dynamically typed languages or loosely typed languages.

Dynamically typed languages receive different types of data over time. Other languages such as Java and C++ are what we normally refer to as statically typed languages as the type of data is already defined at compilation.

According to ECMAScript (ES6), JavaScript support 7 data types. Six of these data types are defined (primitive).

These primitive data types include:

- Numbers
- Booleans
- Strings
- Null
- Undefined
- Time
- Arrays
- JavaScript Objects

Let us discuss JavaScript data types a bit further:

JavaScript Numbers

In JavaScript, Numbers are primitive data types that represent numerical values such as whole numbers (integers) and floating points (decimal values).

As usual, in JavaScript, you do not have to specify the data type to use it.

```
var myNum = 100;
var result = 100 + 200;
```

JavaScript Booleans

In JavaScript, we use Booleans to represent conditional values that evaluate to one of two options: "True" or "False." In JavaScript, to determine whether a value evaluates to true or false, set the Boolean() function against an expression.

For example:

```
<html>
    <body>
        <p>Display the value of Boolean(100 > 80):</p>
        <button onclick="myFunction()">Boolean</button>
        <p id="demo"></p>
    <script>
        function myFunction() {
        document.getElementById("demo").innerHTML = Boolean(100> 80);
        }
    </script>
    </body>
</html>
```

In JavaScript, Booleans have two main properties:

- o Prototype – this property allows addition of methods and properties to objects

JavaScript

- Constructor – This property returns a reference to the Boolean object used to create it.

The supported methods for the Boolean Object include:

- valueOf() – returns original value of the Boolean object.

- toString() – used to return a string of either the two Boolean values (True or False)

Strings in JavaScript

A string is a sequence of characters. The sequence of characters is usually zero or more enclosed using double or single quotes. The quotes surrounding the string must match the first one and the last.

```
var name = "JavaScript";
var lastName = 'ECMA';
var notGood = 'Hello, JS!";
```

JavaScript supports various properties that allow you to work and manipulate strings easily. They include:

- length – used to return the length of the specified string.

- Prototype – similar to Boolean, this property allows addition of properties and methods to the object.

In JavaScript, the methods supported by the string type include:

- concat() – This combines two text of strings to produce one string

JavaScript

- lastIndexOf() – This returns the index of the specified string of the first occurrence. Similar to the indexOf()

- match() – We use this to match an expression against a string

- replace() – We use this to match a string against an expression (and vice versa) and replace the matched substring.

- Search() – This searches for math between an expression and a specific set of string

- Slice() – We use this to extract a section of a specified string to create a new string.

- Split() – This splits the string into an array of strings separated into substrings

- toLowerCase() – We use this to convert a set of strings to lower case. This is similar to the toLocaleLowerCase() that converts the string to lower case according to locale.

- toUpperCase() – This converts a set of string to upper case; it is similar to toLocaleUpperCase()

- valueOf() – This returns a primitive value of a string object.

- Substring() – This returns characters in a specified string between two indexes.

JavaScript

Since in JavaScript we express strings using quotes, it can be confusing to JavaScript if you were to write a sentence as

```
var myString = "The moderator said: "Do not Go looking for him";
```

The above code contains errors. This is because once JavaScript comes across similar quotes as the one used in opening, it assumes that this is the end of the string. This is where we find it necessary to use the escape characters.

We use the back-slash (\) escape character to turn special characters into part of a string. In the above Example, it turns the speech quotation marks into strings.

```
var myString = "The moderator said: \"Do not Go looking for him";
```

If you want to insert a single quote, a double quote, or a backslash into a string, you can use the following escape characters.

- o \" – inserts a double quote into the string
- o \' – inserts a single quote into a string
- o \\ - inserts a backslash into a string

However, JavaScript supports 6 other types of escape characters such as:

- o \b – backspace
- o \f – form feed
- o \n – new line

These are some of the examples. They do not make any sense in HTML and were developed to control teletypes, fax and such.

You can also create Strings as objects. However, do not use Strings as objects as they tend to be slow to execute.

Null in JavaScript

JavaScript supports the "null' data type used to refer to nothing. It means that an object does not exist. We normally use it to represent an intentional absence of an object value.

```
var information = {firstName: "Peter", lastName: "Green", age: 40, location: "USA"};
var information = null;
```

You can learn more about the null data type from the resource page available below:

https://devdocs.io/javascript/global_objects/null

Javascript Undefined

We use the undefined data type to represent a variable that contains no value. It does not represent an empty value. You can either declare a variable and leave it unassigned or assign it to undefined type.

For example, type the following code into your text editor:

```
var myVar; // undefined type
myVar = undefined; // also undefined

// to check for type
typeof(myVar);
```

To check for the data type in JavaScript, use the typeof() method passing the variable as the argument.

You may notice that the null and undefined types appear the same. They are equal as far as value is concerned but different in type.

```
typeof undefined; // undefined;
typeof null // null type;

null == undefined; // evaluates to true - value is equal
null === undefined // evaluates to false; - the type is different
```

Time – JavaScript

JavaScript provides time objects that allow programmers to work with time related aspects such as seconds, minutes, hours, days etc. To get the current date in JavaScript, we use the Date() method.

```
Date() // returns the current data
// assign it the a variable
var today = Date();
typeof(today); // "Sun Aug 25 2019 15:22:46 GMT+0300 (East Africa Time)" - returned as a string
```

From the above example, we can get detailed information such as Date, Time and the Time Format used. Date() function returns the information as a string.

We can also work with other time related information apart from the current time and date. We do this by creating the date object and then specifying the parameters in the date constructor.

JavaScript Arrays

We can define Arrays as a series of grouped data of the same type. Arrays allow storage of multiple values of the same type under one name. This allows you to organize the code and make it more readable.

Suppose you want to store numbers from 1 to 100, instead of creating num1, num2, num3...num100, you can use an array to store these values under a name such as numbers.

The syntax for creating an Array in JavaScript is var <array_name> = new Array(number_of_elements);

Once the array has been initialized, you can access, read, delete and update elements in the array by referencing them using their index. JavaScript is a zero indexed programming language, which means that the first element in the array contains index 0.

```javascript
var myArray = new Array(10);
myArray[0] = 10 // set the index 0 to 10
```

To access or update arrays at specific index, you can use the indexes as shown below.

```javascript
var myArray = new Array(10);
myArray[0] = 10 // set the index 0 to 10

// access the array
myArray[0] // returns the first element in the array
//updating the elements in the array
myArray[9] = 100 // updates element in index 9 to 100
```

JavaScript

Unlike some other programming languages, JavaScript does not support two dimensional arrays. However, you can match the property of a two dimensional array.

Suppose a single dimensional array (discussed above) is visualized as a stack of elements, then, we can emulate the two dimensional array as multicolumn grid. WE can do this by creating an array within an array.

To create an array within an array, we create a single dimensional array and then loop through each item in the array. Creating an index for each column of the grid. A typical example of a two dimensional array could be something similar to this:

```
var names = new Array(3)

for (i=0; i &lt;3; i++)
names[i]=new Array(3)

names[0][1] = "Gren"
names[0][2] = "John"
names[0][3] = "Jane"

names[1][1] = "Mary"
names[1][2] = "Peter"
names[1][3] = "Doe"

names[2][1] = "Lorem"
names[2][2] = "Ipsum"
names[2][3] = "JavaScript"
```

The above example would result into a two dimensional array that looks similar to this:

Gren	John	Jane
Mary	Peter	Doe
Lorem	Ipsum	JavaScirpt

JavaScript Objects

JavaScript objects are very important data type within the language. Objects are usually the building blocks for Modern JavaScript. JavaScript Objects are however different from primitive data types such as Numbers, Strings, and Booleans etc. This is because they store a single value each – i.e. depending on the data type.

On the other hand, objects:

- o Are more complex and can contain any of the primitive data types.
- o Can contain reference data-types.
- o Contain keys that can be a variable or functions also known as properties or methods based on the object context.

JavaScript objects can be defined as unordered set of related data containing primitive data or reference value set with key pairs.

JavaScript

We create objects using the curly braces. The syntax for JavaScript Object creation is as follows:

```
var myObject = {key1: value1, key2:value2, key3:value3}
```

```
let student = {
    name: "Peter Green",
    Country: "USA",
    State: "Texas",
    LogNo: 5698413,
    admDate: "2019"
}
```

From the above example, Name, Country, State, LogNo and admDate all represent keys. On the other hand, the Peter Green, USA, Texas, 5698413 and 2019 all represent the values for each key respectively.

Each of the above keys are referred to as properties of an object.

NOTE: Objects may contain function as a member of the values. This function is mainly referred to as method of the object.

For Example:

```
let placeInfo = {
    name: 'Hannah',
    location : 'South Carolina',
    established : '1971',
    displayInfo : function() {
    console.log(`${placeInfo.name} was established
    in ${placeInfo.established} at ${placeInfo.location}`);
    }
}
placeInfo.displayInfo();
```

40

Property names can also be represented as strings where in this case, the values of the specified properties must be expressed as strings as well.

Inherited Properties

Inherited properties are the properties inherited from the object prototype rather than defined in the object definition – also called as Object's own property. We can find out if the property in the object is OOP (Object Own Propert – Not Objected Oriented Programming) by using the hasOwnProperty() Method.

The Properties on Object Data in JavaScript has four attributes:

- Value – contains the value of the object property

- Enumerable – allows enumeration by the use of for-in if true. If false, the property is referred to as a non-enumerable property.

- Configurable – If this attribute is set to true, it attempts to perform certain actions such as change the property to access-or, delete the property, or change the attributes. Otherwise, these actions will fail.

- Writable – Allows the changing or property values if set to true.

You can learn more about JS Objects from the following invaluable resource page Mozilla Developer Network

Chapter 7: Working with JavaScript Operators

We normally use JavaScript Operators to perform operations on supported data types. Operators perform actions on the given data types and return a different value.

Let us take an example of:

10 * 10 = 100

In the above example, 10 and 10 are operands and the * is the operator. The operator in this case performed multiplication and returned 100 as the result. Like many other programming languages, JavaScript supports different types of operators.

They include:

- Arithmetic Operators
- Assignment Operators
- Comparison Operators
- Boolean/Logical Operators
- Bitwise Operators
- Conditional Operators

We shall now discuss how to work with each type of these JavaScript operators:

Arithmetic Operators

In JavaScript and many other programming languages, we use Arithmetic operators to perform arithmetic operations against given operands. The following shows the supported JavaScript Arithmetic Operators.

JavaScript

Operator	Function
+	Returns Addition of given operands
-	Performs subtraction of two given operands
*	Returns the multiple of two given values
/	Performs division against two given operands
%	Known as modulo, it returns the modulus or the remainder of a division
++	Increment operator returns the a given operand + 1
--	Decrement operator returns the value of a given operand - 1

NOTE: In JavaScript, the addition operator works on both Numeric and String Data types. For Example 10 + 10 = 20 while "10" + "10" = "1010"

Assignment Operators

We use assignment Operators to assign values to a given variable after a specified operation.

The following is the list of supported JavaScript Assignment Operators.

Operator	Function
=	Assigns a given value to a variable
+=	Used to add a value and assign to itself. For example, a+=b is the same as a = a +b
-=	Used to subtract and assign a value between two operands. a-=b is the same as a = a-b
*=	Multiplies and assigns a value. Example a*=b is same as a = a * b
/=	Divides and assigns a value. a/=b is same as a = a / b
%=	Used to perform modulus and assign a value. a%=b is same as a = a % b

NOTE: Do not override the assigned variable; otherwise, you might get an error.

```
var a = 34;
var b = 17;

a+=b // 51
//variable value reassign
a-=b // above function sets a = 51 thus = 34;
```

Comparison Operators

In JavaScript, we use Comparison Operators to compare given operators against a certain condition.

The following is the list of supported Comparison Operators in JavaScript.

Operator	Function
==	Compares two operands for equality and returns a Boolean value
===	Identity operator is used to check for identity between two operands
!=	Is not equal to – 5 != 5 returns false. 10!=30 returns true
!===	Non identical
<	Less than between two operands.
<=	Less than or equal to
>	Greater than
>=	Greater than or equal to

Boolean/Logical Operators

We normally use Logical Operators to perform logical comparison between two or more operands and expressions. We usually use them to combine two or more conditions.

JavaScript supports the Following Logical operators.

Operator	Function
&&	Logical AND is used to test for no-zero values between two operands. I.e. Both conditions must evaluate to true.
||	Logical OR is used to test if either of the conditions is true. If one condition is true, the condition is set to true
!	Logical NOT is used to reverse the result of a Boolean condition.

Bitwise Operators

JavaScript support the following kinds of bitwise operators.

Operator	Function
&	Bitwise AND – performs a logical AND comparison per bit
|	Bitwise OR – performs a logical OR comparison per each bit
^	Performs an exclusive Boolean OR comparison per each bit
~	Functions by reversing each bit in an operand
>>	Binary Right Shift Operator
<<	Binary Left Shift operator – shifts all the bits in first operand to the left by number of places in

JavaScript

	the second operand.
>>>	Binary Right Shift with Zero – performs similar to >> except the left shifted bit are always zero

Conditional Operators

The conditional operator is also known as ternary operator. It is the only operator supported by JavaScript that accepts 3 operands. You can consider it a shortcut for the if statement (discussed later). The basic syntax for a ternary operation in JavaScript is:

```
condition     ?     expression_If_True     : expression_If_False
```

Let us explore the above syntax.

- The `condition-` is set to the expression that is being used as a condition.

- Expression_If_True – expression to be evaluated if the condition is evaluated to true.

- Expression_If_True – expression to be evaluated if the condition is evaluated to false.

JavaScript

Example:

```javascript
var age = 26;
var visit = (age >= 21) ? "Bar" : "Restruarant";
console.log(visit);
```

Chapter 8: Working with JavaScript Conditionals

We use JavaScript conditionals to perform a specific action if a certain condition is achieved. JavaScript supports conditional control flow using the if...else statements.

The following is a list of conditionals in JavaScript:

- If
- If...else
- Else if

If Conditions

In JavaScript, the if condition is very straight forward. It executes a set of code with a block if a condition is evaluated to true.

The syntax for if statement is:

```
If (condition)

{

// execute this block of code;

}
```

Example:

JavaScript

```
var score = 80;
if (score >= 80) {
    console.log("Passed");
}
if (score < 80) {
    console.log("Failed");
}
```

From the above example, the first if control condition contains an expression (score >= 80) as the condition. If the condition is evaluated to true, (in this case it is), the message "Passed" is printed on the screen. If not, the condition in the second expression will be executed.

NOTE: if the line of code to be executed is one, curly braces are not required.

If...Else

The **if** condition above proves useful if you want to perform an action if the condition is true. This does not come in handy when you want to perform another action if the condition is false. This is where the **else** condition comes in handy. The syntax for the **if...else** statement is:

```
If (condition) {

// execute this code;

}

Else {

// execute this instead;
```

}

We can implement the above example to test the score of a student as shown below.

```
var score = 80;
if (score >= 80) {
    console.log("Score Above 80");
}
else {
    console.log("Score is Below 80");
}
```

The else condition allows an action to be performed if the expression in the first block is evaluated to true instead of stopping the execution.

Else...if

The other control flow supported by JavaScript is the else...if statement. It is the most powerful of the two above as it allows the code to check for multiple conditions until a condition evaluates to true.

The syntax for this control statement is as follows:

```
If (condition1) {

// execute this;

}

Else if (condition2) {

// execute this
```

JavaScript

```
}

Else if (condition3) {

//execute this;

}

Else {

// execute this if all other conditions are false

}
```

We can implement the score test program using various criteria.

```javascript
var socre = 80;
if (score <= 30) {
    console.log("Failed");
}
else if(score >= 50) {
    console.log("Average");
}
else if (score >= 70) {
    console.log("Above Average");
}
else {
    console.log("Excellent");
}
```

JavaScript Switch

JavaScript switch statements are very powerful control statements that you can use to check multiple conditions. For example, using the score example above, if the score is 40, we can perform a condition for each. We can use the switch statement for this case.

The JavaScript syntax for the switch statement is as follows:

```
Switch (expression) {

Case 1;

    //execute this code

    Break;

Case 2;

    // execute this code

    Break;

Case n;

    //  execute this code.

    Break;

Default;

    // if all above cases evaluate to false

    // default condition.
```

JavaScript

From the above syntax, the switch statement contains the literal value or an expression. Once the expression has been executed and returns a value, the case that contains the returned value is executed. If none of cases matches, the default condition is executed.

NOTE: Use the break keyword to stop and exit the current switch statement.

```javascript
var socre = 80;
switch(score) {
    case 40:
        console.log("Failed");
        break;
    case 50:
        console.log("Average");
        break;
    case 70:
        console.log("Above Average");
        break;
    case 80:
        console.log("Passsed");
        break;
    default:
        console.log("Default Value");
}
```

Chapter 9: Working with JavaScript Loops

In programming, we use loops to perform a specific set of actions until a condition is met. Loops are a very powerful aspect of computer programming and almost any programming language supports them.

Loops contain three main aspects.

- Initializer – initializes the counter variable e.g. a = 1;
- Condition – sets the condition for evaluation e.g. a > 10;
- Iterator – updates the counter per iteration e.g. a++;

Like most programming languages, JavaScript has two loops:

- For Loops
- While loop

JavaScript For Loops

The for loop is the most widely used form of loop in programming. It involves all the three features discussed above. The syntax for a JavaScript is:

```
for (initialization; condition; iterator;) {
    // execute this block of code
}
```

The following is an example of a for loop to display the numbers between 1 and 10. Not including 10.

JavaScript

```
var count;

for (count = 0; count < 10; count++) {
    console.log(count);
}
```

From the above example, we can see that count is initially set to 0. When the condition is checked, it evaluates to true and the number 0 is printed. The count is then updated and becomes 1. This process continues as the value of count increases on each run. This value however reaches 10 and the value 10 < 10 becomes false thus terminating the loop.

JavaScript While Loops

JavaScript also supports a while loop that allows a specific code to be run until a set condition is false. Unlike for loop, a while loop requires the condition and not initialization and iteration.

JavaScript

The syntax for JavaScript while loop is:

```
While (condition) {

    // execute this code

    // iteration updater

}
```

```
var count = 0;
while (count < 10) {
    console.log(count);
    count++;
}
```

Do...While Loops

JavaScript also allows the use of do while loop. This type of loop is similar to the while loop except that it runs the condition expression after running the block of code. This means that even if the condition never evaluates to true, the line of code inside the do while will run at least once.

The syntax for a do...while loop is:

```
do {

    // execute this code;

}
While (condition)
```

JavaScript

```
var count = 0;
do {
    console.log(count);
    count++;
} while (count < 10)
```

NOTE: To avoid creating a loop that never ends (infinite loop), Always ensure that your loop condition eventually evaluates to false.

Chapter 10: Working with JavaScript Functions

A **function** in programming or also known as **a method** (in some programming languages) is group of code that performs a specific action and returns a value. It is reusable code and efficient for large programs. It helps in modularizing the code and avoids code repetition.

JavaScript, just like other programming languages allows for us to write our own functions. An example of built in function is alert() or log(). In this section, we are going to see how to write our own functions in JavaScript.

Function Definition

Before using a function, you first have to define it. We define JavaScript functions using the keyword function, followed by the function name. The full syntax of function definition is:

```
Function <function-name> (parameters) {
    // function code
};
```

Below is an example of a function that prints "Hello World".

```
function printHello() {
    console.log("Hello Wolrd");
}
```

Function Calls

Once you define the function, you can use the function by calling it anywhere in the program. For example, to use the printHello() fuction above, we use printHello();

```
function printHello() {
    console.log("Hello Wolrd");
}
printHello();
```

Function Parameters

In JavaScript, you can create functions that accept arguments or none. Let us see how to write functions with parameters. The required parameters of a function are created in the function definition and passed during the function call.

A function can take two or more parameters separated by commas. If you pass more parameters during function call, the others are ignored. In the case of less parameters than required, the value is set to undefined.

Here is an example to calculate the maximum number.

```
function maxValue(num1, num2) {
    var max;
    if (num1 > num2) {
        max = num1;
    } else {
        max = num2;
    }
    return max;
}
console.log(maxValue(10,20));
```

JavaScript

NOTE: Since JavaScript is a dynamic scripting language, the parameters can be of any time as long as they do not conflict with program operation.

Return Value

JavaScript has a return keyword used in functions to return a value after the function computation. The return keyword should be the last statement in a function. In the above example, after computing the max value, we return it and print on the screen.

JavaScript Nested Functions

JavaScript supports the capability of a function to contain inner functions within it. Each nested function is usually within the scope of the outer function. This means that each inner function can access variables and values of the outer function while the outer function cannot access the inner.

```javascript
function printHello(name)
{
    function greet() {
        console.log(("Hey " + name));
    }
    return greet();
}
printHello("Sammy");
```

You can have as many nested function as required. Ensure the functions do not conflict others due to scope of each function.

Anonymous Functions

JavaScript allows the use of functions without a name. A function of this kind is known as an anonymous function. Anonymous functions are mainly used to pass callback functions or invoke a function expression. Anonymous functions however must be assigned to variables. Example of an anonymous function is below.

```javascript
var talk = function (){
    console.log(("Hello World!"));
};

talk();

var sayHey = function (name) {
    console.log(("Hello " + name));
};

talk();
sayHey("James");
```

Chapter 11: Working with JavaScript Events

JavaScript is the language used to interact with HTML and CSS in a web page. In web programming, HTML is often regarded as the Noun, CSS the adjective, and JavaScript as verb. Interaction of JavaScript and HTML occurs using events. In this section, we are going to look at how to use events to work with HTML and JavaScript.

In a webpage, events can range from loading of the page to the complex computations required to run a vibrant webpage. When you click a button and it performs a specific action, this is a JavaScript event.

Events are part of the Document Object Model (discussed later) with each element containing set of JavaScript events.

Onclick Event

This is the most popular type of JavaScript event. This event activates when the user clicks a certain part of the page using activation mouse click.

For example, let us create a simple web page and include a JavaScript event that is triggered once the button is clicked.

JavaScript

```
<html>
    <head>
        <script type = "text/javascript">
            <!--
            function Hello() {
                alert("Hello, Welcome to JavaScript Events")
            }
        </script>
    </head>

    <body>
        <p>Click Here</p>
        <form>
            <input type = "button" onclick = "Hello()" value = "Hello" />
        </form>
    </body>
</html>
```

If you open the above page and click on the button, a message box with the string "Hello, Welcome to JavaScript Events" is displayed.

OnMouseOver and onMouseOut Events

These two common types of events are mainly used to create effects on images in a web page. The onmouseover event is triggered once the mouse reaches the part of the web page. Onmouseout acts as the opposite of onmouseover which deactivates the event created.

JavaScript

HTML5 and JavaScript interact on various events. The table below contains the most common and useful JavaScript events.

Event	Action / Trigger
onclick	Activates on mouse click
oncontextmenu	Activates on context menu
onload	Activated when the document is loaded
onforminput	Activated when form accepts input from the user.
oninvalid	Activates on invalid HTML element
onfocus	Activates on window focus
onerror	Triggers on error occurrence

JavaScript

onkeydown	Activates on key press
onkeyup	Activates on key press – similar to onkeyup
onsubmit	Triggered on HTML form submit request
onselect	Activates on html element selection
ontimeupdate	Activates on media play time change
onpause	Triggers on media pause
onplay	Activates when media data starts playing

JavaScript has many other types of events each performing a specific task upon a specific action. Reference here for the comprehensive list:

https://mzl.la/1JcBR22

Chapter 12: About Different Types of Errors & JavaScript Error Handling

In programming, errors are a common happenstance and it's very likely that any of the program code you write will have errors. JavaScript is a dynamic language that offers a dynamic way to deal with errors.

Let us begin learning how to handle errors in JavaScript by discussing the types of errors that are likely to occur within a program.

Types of Program Errors

The following are the most common types of program errors:

Syntax Errors

Syntax errors occur during interpretation segment of a JavaScript program. They are also known as parsing-errors. They are mainly caused by misusing the JavaScript syntax.

For example:

```
var hello = "Hello world";
console.log(;;|
```

In JavaScript, a syntax error does not affect other parts of the program provided they do not rely on the part with an error.

Runtime Errors

Runtime Errors are errors that occur during interpretation or compilation of the program. They are mainly known as exceptions. An example of runtime error would be calling a function that does not exist.

For example:

```
var hello = "Hello world";
console.log(hello);

uName(name, hello); // error
```

Similar to syntax errors, they only affect the thread which they appear allowing execution of other parts of the program.

Logical Errors

Logical Errors are type of errors that result in program not working as expected. They mainly affect the logical performance of the program. They are very hard to track since they neither occur from runtime or syntax errors. Logical errors usually take up to 90% of program's debugging work/process.

The JavaScript Error Handling Mechanism

Like most programming languages, JavaScript offers a way to anticipate errors that may occur in the program and solve it before it happens. The error handling mechanism is only effective to some types of errors. Using the **try**...**catch**...**finally** statements.

The syntax for this mechanism is:

```
try {
    // code that may result in an error
}
Catch {
    // if an error occurs, run this code
}
Finally {
    // if error occurs or not, run this code
}
```

Let us discuss the code above:

- Try – In this example, we have used the try keyword to set the block of code anticipated to result into an error.

- Catch – We have used this to set the block of code that handles the errors if it occurs. In most situations, we use this to report the error to the user or the developers.

- Finally – We use this keyword to set the block of code that executes whether the error occurs or not. You can use it to reset the try block to default.

```
try
{
    var result = Sum(10, 20); // undefined function
}
catch(ex)
{
    document.getElementById("errorMessage").innerHTML = ex;
}
finally{
    document.getElementById("message").innerHTML = "I will always be executed";
}
```

JavaScript Throw Statement

In JavaScript, we use the throw statement to create your own customized exceptions or raise JavaScript built-in exceptions.

```
<html>
<body>
    <h1>Throw Statement</h1>

    <p id="errorMessage"></p>

    <script>
        try
        {
            throw "Error occurred";
        }
        catch(ex)
        {
            document.getElementById("errorMessage").innerHTML = ex;
        }
    </script>
</body>
</html>
```

Chapter 13: JavaScript's Document Object Model

Web pages displayed on a browser window can be considered as objects. A Document object shows the HTML document displayed in that window. The Document object contains a range of properties used to refer to other objects allowing access and modification of document objects. The access and modification of the document objects is done using a particular way referred to as Document Object Model or DOM. These document objects are represented in a hierarchical manner.

If you are familiar with advanced HTML, you know that the HTML DOM defines:

- HTML elements
- Methods for HTML elements
- Events for HTML elements
- Properties for HTML elements

The HTML DOM is a JavaScript Programming Interface (API) that allows JavaScript to:

- Modify HTML elements
- Modify HTML attributes
- React to HTML events
- Modify HTML events

- Modify CSS styles

There are several types of DOMs. They include:

- The Legacy DOM –Introduced in earlier versions of JavaScript, this DOM allows access to specific key elements in the HTML documents. These elements include forms and images. Every browser in existence supports this DOM.

- The W3C DOM – This type of DOM is standardized by the World Wide Web Consortium (W3C). It allows access to and modification of all elements in the HTML documents. All modern browsers support this model.

- The IE4 DOM – This type of DOM model was introduced for certain version of Microsoft Internet Explorer. Its use is not very common.

In this section, we are going to focus on using the W3C DOM model. The hierarchical representation of the DOM is below.

JavaScript

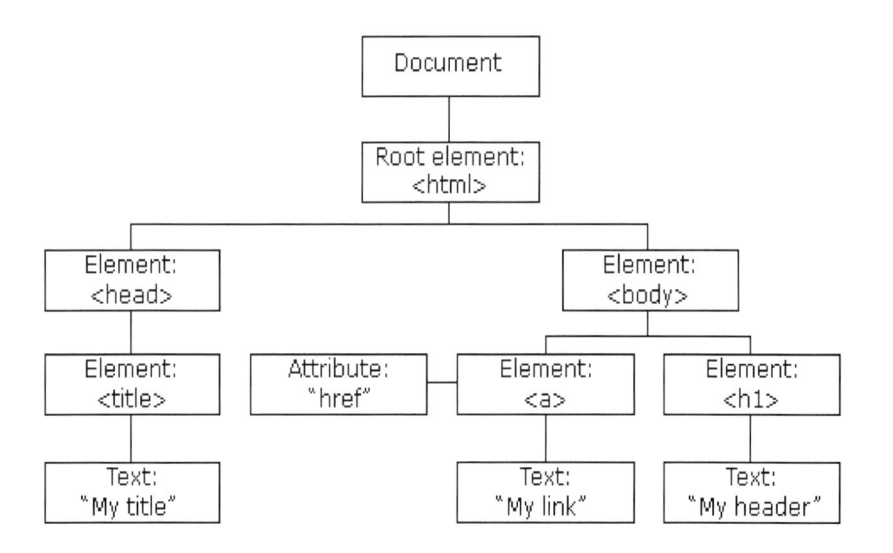

```
                    Document
                        |
                  Root element:
                    <html>
                   /        \
         Element:            Element:
         <head>              <body>
         /                   /        \
   Element:  Attribute:  Element:   Element:
   <title>   "href"      <a>        <h1>
      |                    |          |
   Text:                Text:       Text:
   "My title"          "My link"   "My header"
```

The W3C DOM has three main parts:

- HTML DOM – standard DOM model for HTML documents
- Core DOM – the standard model for all web document types
- XML DOM – standard DOM for XML documents

DOM Methods

The html DOM elements allows for manipulation and addition of events on HTML elements. The HTML DOM properties on the other hand are values in html elements that can be modified.

Example:

JavaScript

```
<html>
<body>

<h2>DOM Manipulation</h2>

<p id="p1">Hello, Welcome to DOM Manipulation</p>

<script>
document.getElementById("p1").innerHTML = "Hello World!";
</script>

</body>
</html>
```

In the above example, we are modifying the content of the <p> element using the innerHTML with the id "p1". From the above example, we can see that the getElementtById is a method while innerHTML is the property. The innerHTML property can help modify any HTML element within it.

DOM Document Object

The document object in the HTML DOM is responsible for all other objects. In other words, other objects reside the Document object itself. We normally use it to represent the entire web page in it.

Let us look at some ways in which you can use the document object to manipulate elements within the document.

Selecting HTML Elements

There are various methods you can use to select an element in the DOM.

Let us look at some of the commonly used:

79

- document.getElementById (id) – used to select a HTML element using its assigned id.

- document.elementsByClassName(class_name) – Used to select items using their class Names.

- document.elementsByTagName(tag_name) – selects elements by their respective tag names.

Deleting and Adding HTML elements

We can also use the document methods to remove and delete elements within it. It also allows us to replace the existing elements. Let us see how we can do this.

- Document.removeChild(html element) – Deletes the specified html element.

- Document.createElement(element tag) – creates new specified element within the document.

- Document.replaceChild(new_element, old_element) – replaces an existing html element with a new specified one.

Manipulating HTML elements

To manipulate HTML elements:

- element.innerHTML = new html content – used to chnage the contents of an html element.

- element.attribute = new value – used to change the attribute of an html element.

- element.style.property = new style – used to change the set HTML element styles

- element.setAttribute(attribute, value) – used to change the html attribute value of an element

Event Handlers

We can also add events to the specified html elements. These methods are triggered and activated once the action is executed.

Document.getElementById(id).(event) = function(call) {//run some code}

These types of event triggers are not mostly used but some people prefer them as they are conventional.

NOTE: JavaScript has various other object methods, collection, and properties.

Chapter 14: Asynchronous JavaScript and XML (AJAX)

Asynchronous JavaScript —let's just call it AJAX— is a new technology used to create interactive and faster web applications. It relies on HTML, CSS, JavaScript, and XML.

Here are some of the features that make AJAX worth learning about:

- o It is user friendly
- o It provides an amazing UI for web applications
- o Easy and Simple to implement
- o Supports Data view control
- o Allows Live Data Binding
- o Increases web application speed
- o It offers cross browser support
- o It is server independent
- o Allows for asynchronous communications
- o Minimizes bandwidth usage
- o Provides great client template rendering
- o Does not required heavy server resources

As you can see, AJAX is a developer's dream that makes the web development process fun and interactive. Even advanced tech giants such as YouTube, Twitter, Google and Facebook, among many other utilizes AJAX.

AJAX has some disadvantages such as:

- Security – allows users to view the AJAX source code used.
- Search engines indexing – Ajax websites are less likely to be indexed by search engines such as Google.
- Brings network latency problems.

In this section, we are going to see how JavaScript relates to AJAX.

XMLHttpRequest Object – Ajax

Ajax relies a lot on JavaScript and more importantly, the DOM. In this section we are going to discuss a technology that Ajax utilizes: **XMLHttpRequest**

XMLHttpRequest is a JavaScript object that carries out asynchronous interactive requests with the server. We can also define it as an API used by web scripting languages to transfer and manipulate data to and from the server.

It is responsible for performing several operations such as:

- o Receives data from the server in various formats such as JSON and plain text.
- o Responsible for page updates without reload
- o Sends the data to the server from the client silently

XMLHttpRequest Methods

This object offers some methods and properties that we need to get familiar with.

In this section, we are going to focus on the important ones.

- o Send() – used to send a request
- o setRequestHeader(label, value) – appends a label/value pair to the HTTP header being sent.
- o abort() – used to cancel ongoing requests

- getAllResponseHeaders() – used to acquire all set of HTTP headers and return them as a string.

- Open(method, url) - opens the request by stipulating the post or get method and url.

- Open(method, url, async, username, password) – opens a request similar to the one above specifying whether asynchronous or not, username and password.

XMLHttpRequest Properties

The following are the properties of the XMLHttpRequest Object properties:

- Readystate – used to define the current state of the XMLHttpRequest object. This property contains several values to denote the state:
  - 0 – before request initialization
  - 1 – already setup request
  - 2 – sent request
  - 3 – request in process
  - 4 – request completed

- Onreadystatechange – acts as an event handler for events that are triggered after every state change

- responseText – returns the server response as a string.

JavaScript

- responseXML – similar to responseText but returns the response as an XML object.
- Status – returns the server status in numerical value. e.g. "404 – NOT FOUND"
- statusText – returns the status as a string

The syntax for creating the XMLHttpRequest object in modern browsers is:

```
var variableName = new XMLHttpRequest();
```

Chapter 15: Forms and Form Validations Using JavaScript

If you are familiar with HTML and HTML forms, it will be easy to understand how form validations work. Form validations used to be performed on the server once the user has provided the data and submitted. Once the data has been checked on the server and errors found, the server would send all the data back to the user with resubmission request. This used a lot of server resources and took a long time.

Form validation using JavaScript allows the information being provided by the client to be checked before submission to the server. It performs two main functions:

- Basic Form Validation – this function makes sure all the compulsory form fields are provided.

- Data Format Validation – This function checks for logic and value in the data provided. For example, an email must have the @ symbol and such.

Let us look at how to implement these two functions in HTML forms

Basic Form Validation

Let us see how to implement the basic form validation using the validate() function upon the onsubmit event. This ensures that when the client clicks the submit button, it will check if all the data is provided.

```
<script>
    // Form validation code will come here.
    function validate() {

        if( document.myForm.Name.value == "" ) {
            alert( "Enter Your Name" );
            document.myForm.Name.focus() ;
            return false;
        }
        if( document.myForm.EMail.value == "" ) {
            alert( "Enter Your Name:" );
            document.myForm.EMail.focus() ;
            return false;
        }
        if( document.myForm.Zip.value == "" || isNaN( document.myForm.Zip.value ) ||
            document.myForm.Zip.value.length != 5 ) {

            alert( "Please provide a zip in the format #####." );
            document.myForm.Zip.focus() ;
            return false;
        }
        return( true );
    }
</script>
```

Data Form Validation

In this part, we are going to validate the correct email address in the form. The logic is, the email must contain an @ symbol and a dot. Also, the first character must not be a symbol and there must be a character after the @ sign.

```
<script>
    <!--
        function validateEmail() {
            var emailID = document.myForm.EMail.value;
            atpos = emailID.indexOf("@");
            dotpos = emailID.lastIndexOf(".");

            if (atpos < 1 || ( dotpos - atpos < 2 )) {
                alert("Please provide a valid email address: ")
                document.myForm.EMail.focus() ;
                return false;
            }
            return( true );
        }
    //-->
</script>
```

JavaScript

NOTE: The above is a section of an html web page. To create such a page, you need HTML forms knowledge.

Chapter 16: JavaScript Project: Step By Step Process to Create the Color Game

In this chapter of the guide, we are going to create a color game project using HTML, CSS and JavaScript. The game uses RGB color code and allows the user to select the matching color using the RGB code given.

This is an interactive project and the Knowledge we have discussed above about HTML and CSS will not apply, as this is a JavaScript only project. To find more information about RGB color codes, you can visit the following resource page:

https://bit.ly/1eowhM9

The project is systematic and utilizes a lot of JavaScript and DOM manipulation.

Step 1

Create html and CSS files and name them index.html and style.css respectively.

Step 2

Using your JavaScript environment, edit your index html file by entering the following code.

JavaScript

```html
<html>
<head>
    <title>Color Guess Game</title>
    <link rel="stylesheet" type="text/css" href="style.css">
    <link href="https://fonts.googleapis.com/css?family=Open+Sans|Roboto&display=swap" rel="stylesheet">
</head>
<body>
    <h1>
        <br>
        <span id="colorDisplay">RGB</span>
        <br>
COLOR GAME
```

```html
    </h1>
    <div id="stripe">
        <button id="reset">New Colors</button>
        <span id="message"></span>
        <button class="mode">Easy</button>
        <button class="mode selected">Advanced</button>
    </div>
    <div id="container">
        <div class="square"></div>
        <div class="square"></div>
        <div class="square"></div>
        <div class="square"></div>
        <div class="square"></div>
    </div>
<script type="text/javascript" src="index.js"></script>
</body>
</html>
```

NOTE: In the above code, we start by setting the title and head, next we set the fonts using the Google font API, and then we link the required CSS file and JavaScript file in the bottom.

Step 3

Next, open and edit the style.css file and set the code as follows:

```css
body {
    background-color: #232323;
    margin: 0;
    font-family: 'Roboto', sans-serif;
}


h1 {
    text-align: center;
    line-height: 1.1;
    font-weight: normal;
    color: white;
    background-color: steelblue;
    margin: 0;
    text-transform: uppercase;
    padding: 20px 0;
}
```

```
#colorDisplay {

    font-size: 200%;

}


#message {

    display: inline-block;

    width: 20%;

}


#container {
```

JavaScript

```
        margin: 20px auto;

        max-width: 600px;

}


.square {

        width: 30%;

        background-color: purple;

        padding-bottom: 30%;

        float: left;

        margin: 1.66%;

        border-radius: 15%;

        transition: background 0.4s;

        --webkit-tranition: background 0.4s;

        --moz-tranition: background 0.4s;

    cursor: pointer;

}
```

```
#stripe {

    background-color: white;

    height: 30px;

    text-align: center;

}


.selected {

    color: white;

    background: steelblue;

}
```

JavaScript

```css
button {
    border: none;
    background: none;
    text-transform: uppercase;
    height: 100%;
    font-weight: 700;
    color: steelblue;
    letter-spacing: 1px;
    font-size: inherit;
    transition: all 0.3s;
    --webkit-tranition: all 0.3s;
    --moz-tranition: all 0.3s;
    outline: none;
}

button:hover {
    color: white;
    background: steelblue;
}
```

Step 4

The next thing we need to do is to create the required JavaScript file and name it index.js.

Enter the following code below:

```javascript
var numSquares = 6;

var colors = [];

var pickedColor;

var squares = document.querySelectorAll(".square");

var colorDisplay = document.getElementById("colorDisplay");

var messageDisplay = document.querySelector("#message");

var h1 = document.querySelector("h1");

var resetButton = document.querySelector("#reset");

var modeButtons = document.querySelectorAll(".mode");


init();
```

JavaScript

```
function init(){

    setupModeButtons();

    setupSquares();

    reset();

}


function setupModeButtons(){

    for(var i = 0; i < modeButtons.length; i++){

        modeButtons[i].addEventListener("click", function(){

    modeButtons[0].classList.remove("selected");
```

JavaScript

```
        modeButtons[1].classList.remove("selected");

            this.classList.add("selected");

            this.textContent === "Easy" ? numSquares = 3: numSquares = 6;

            reset();

        });

    }

}


function setupSquares(){

    for(var i = 0; i < squares.length; i++){

    //add click listeners to squares

        squares[i].addEventListener("click", function(){

            //grab color of clicked square
```

JavaScript

```
        var clickedColor = this.style.background;
        //compare color to pickedColor
        if(clickedColor === pickedColor){
                messageDisplay.textContent      =   "Correct!";
                resetButton.textContent   =    "Play Again?"
                changeColors(clickedColor);
                h1.style.background = clickedColor;
        } else {
                this.style.background = "#232323";
                messageDisplay.textContent    =    "Try Again"
        }
```

JavaScript

```
        });

    }

}


function reset(){

    colors = generateRandomColors(numSquares);

    //pick a new random color from array

    pickedColor = pickColor();

    //change colorDisplay to match picked Color

    colorDisplay.textContent = pickedColor;

    resetButton.textContent = "New Colors"

    messageDisplay.textContent = "";

    //change colors of squares

    for(var i = 0; i < squares.length; i++){

        if(colors[i]){

            squares[i].style.display = "block"
```

JavaScript

```
            squares[i].style.background = colors[i];
        } else {
            squares[i].style.display = "none";
        }
    }
    h1.style.background = "steelblue";
}


resetButton.addEventListener("click", function(){
    reset();
})
```

JavaScript

```javascript
function changeColors(color){
    //loop through all squares
    for(var i = 0; i < squares.length; i++){
        //change each color to match given color
        squares[i].style.background = color;
    }
}


function pickColor(){
    var random = Math.floor(Math.random() * colors.length);
    return colors[random];
}
```

JavaScript

```javascript
function generateRandomColors(num){
    //make an array
    var arr = []
    //repeat num times
    for(var i = 0; i < num; i++){
        //get random color and push into arr
        arr.push(randomColor())
    }
    //return that array
    return arr;
}

function randomColor(){
```

JavaScript

```javascript
//pick a "red" from 0 - 255
var r = Math.floor(Math.random() * 256);
//pick a "green" from 0 -255
var g = Math.floor(Math.random() * 256);
//pick a "blue" from 0 -255
var b = Math.floor(Math.random() * 256);
return "rgb(" + r + ", " + g + ", " + b + ")";
}
```

NOTE: Do NOT copy-paste the code. Type it manually as doing so will give you a greater understanding of the JavaScript programming Language and equip you with working knowledge of how to work with JavaScript within the programming environment you set up earlier.

The JavaScript code above adds logic and event to the contents created in the HTML and CSS files. As you have learned, RGB color codes range from 0 to 255. We use this mechanism to generate random colors between 0 and 255. We then ask the user to guess the color generated. If the answer is right, all the squares changes to the correct color; otherwise, the user has to keep guessing. We also add logic such as button click, try again and level selection. The JavaScript code is arranged in sections as to what it accomplishes.

Conclusion

We have come to the end of the book. Thank you for reading and congratulations for reading until the end.

Thank you for reading this JavaScript guide for beginners and intermediates. If you consistently practice what you have learned, you will master JavaScript in no time.

If you found the book valuable, can you recommend it to others? One way to do that is to post a review on Amazon.

Please post a review of this book on Amazon!

Thank you and good luck!

Check Out My Other Books

If you want to expand your knowledge on the world of programming languages, make sure to check out my other books. You can also visit my author page for an updated list of my latest books on various programming languages.

I'm sure you will find them valuable:

[Kali Linux: Kali Linux Made Easy For Beginners And Intermediates Step By Step With Hands On Projects (Including Hacking and Cybersecurity Basics with Kali Linux)](#)

Printed in Great Britain
by Amazon